RETIREMENT
AND FINANCES

SARAH PENNELLS
AND
MARC ROBINSON

LONDON, NEW YORK, MUNICH,
MELBOURNE, DELHI

Project Editor Richard Gilbert
Senior Art Editor Sarah Cowley

DTP Designer Rajen Shah
Production Controller Sarah Sherlock

Managing Editor Adèle Hayward
Managing Art Editor Marianne Markham
Category Publisher Stephanie Jackson

Produced for Dorling Kindersley by
PORTAL PUBLISHING
43 Stanley Street, Brighton
East Sussex BN2 0GP

Creative Director Caroline Marklew
Editorial Director Lorraine Turner

First published in Great Britain in 2003
by Dorling Kindersley Limited,
80 Strand, London WC2R 0RL

A Penguin company

2 4 6 8 10 9 7 5 3 1

Copyright © 2003
Dorling Kindersley Limited, London

Text copyright © 2003
Sarah Pennells
and Marc Robinson

A CIP catalogue record for this book is available
from the British Library

ISBN 0 7513 3724 2

Reproduced by Colourscan, Singapore
Printed in Hong Kong by Wing King Tong

See our complete catalogue at
www.dk.com

CONTENTS

INTRODUCTION

Being able to ignore the alarm clock and give up the nine-to-five routine is only a dream for most of us. However, when you have retired, it is your opportunity to do just that, when you – and not your boss – are in control of your time. You may have plans to globetrot your way through retirement, or maybe you would rather stay closer to home and spend more time with family and friends. Whatever you choose, you need to plan for it in the best way possible. Retirement and Finances will help you take control of your finances: it will tell you about different investment options, how to plan, and where to go for help. Using the techniques in this book, you will ensure that your money carries on working hard when your own working days are over.

5

GETTING STARTED

Many people view retirement either as a chance to relax or to fulfil ambitions. While you may not have enough money to do everything you want, you can make the most of what you have.

CALCULATING WHAT IT WILL TAKE TO RETIRE

Many retired people expect to live on around two-thirds of the income they received while working. You may want more – or less – than that, but keeping a figure in mind will help your planning.

MAKING YOUR FUNDS LAST

At the very least, your goal is to be able to spend what you need and make your money last the rest of your life. There are three basic ways you can make your money last:
- Protect what you have.
- Generate income.
- Grow your assets.

INCREASING LIFE EXPECTANCY

The evidence for increasing life expectancy is clear. Figures by the Continuous Mortality Investigations Bureau at the Institute of Actuaries show that, in 1980, a 35-year-old man could expect to live for an average of 80 years and one month. By 1999 that figure had increased to 85 years and one month. Female life expectancy is increasing more slowly: in 1980, a 35-year-old woman could expect to live for 84 years and seven months; by 1999 the figure was 88 years and one month. As a result, we now need to save more money for our retirement.

ASSESSING LONGEVITY

Here are some factors that affect longevity:

● Ability to deal with stress.
● Family history and genes.
● Exercise.
● Eating habits.
● Weight.
● Income levels.
● Attitude.

CONSIDERING HEALTH

Even if you are putting much younger people to shame in the gym, good health comes with no guarantees. One of the side effects of people living longer is that more people need ongoing nursing care, whether it is in a retirement home or in their own home. Long-term care can be very expensive, and state support is not available to everyone.

EXPLORING TODAY'S POPULATION

Recent research by the Department of Work and Pensions has shown that around 38% of retired people are living solely on the state pension. Of today's working population, around 52% have an occupational or company pension and 19% have a personal pension.

TAKING INFLATION INTO ACCOUNT

Even at a modest rate of inflation, maintaining your lifestyle will cost more each year. Over 20 years, with inflation at 2.5%, the buying power of £1,000 will be reduced to around £600 – and inflation has been much higher in the past.

▼ MAKING YOUR WISHES COME TRUE
A good retirement plan may not be as magical as a genie, but it can help make your dreams come true more effectively than just making wishes.

CHOOSING YOUR FUTURE LIFESTYLE

R etirement lifestyles come with different price tags. Golfing every day or travelling to exotic places will cost a lot more than the retirement dreams of someone who wants only a satellite dish and a remote control. Part of managing your money in retirement involves making key decisions about what your lifestyle will be. Here are several factors to consider.

DECIDING WHERE TO LIVE

You should decide whether you want to stay in your present home for as long as possible or whether you prefer to live out your days somewhere else. Keep in mind that the place where you holiday every year is not necessarily the best place to retire. You may have visited that area only during the most desirable time of year and have not seen it during the off-season. If you plan to work part-time or do voluntary work, make sure those types of opportunities exist in the area you are considering.

THINGS TO KNOW

● Planned communities, such as mobile home parks for retired people, are not for everyone. You may find restrictions on how you can use your property, so read the community's rules and regulations before buying.

PLANNING WHAT TO DO IN RETIREMENT

If you are happy only when you are working, retirement may be a terrible disappointment. Map out your idea of a perfect day. If you love to travel, think about where you want to go and how to control the cost of those trips. Write down a list of hobbies and activities you have always wanted to try. If you already have a hobby, think about turning it into a business. Opening a small business in retirement can help you make the transition from a full-time job. It can also provide tax breaks and bring in a little extra money.

If you find that retirement is not living up to your expectations so far, shift directions. Sit down with your spouse or partner and plot your next moves. If you are in a rut, you can do something different today and head off in a new direction.

SELECTING THE SIZE OF YOUR HOME

There is no reason why you should have to sell up simply because you have retired, but the property you live in at the moment may not be practical. Perhaps you like the city where you are living now, but your home is too big or the stairs seem to get steeper each year. Maybe it is time to buy a smaller home – or something with no stairs at all. You may want to move nearer to children and grandchildren, or you may be perfectly happy where you are. If you are buying something smaller, the chances are you will have some money left over, either to save or to spend on some extras that will make your home-life a little more comfortable. Do not feel pressured into putting your home up for sale, but if it is no longer suitable for your retirement lifestyle, you would be better advised to find something that will suit you better.

SAVING ENOUGH FOR RETIREMENT

One leading insurance company in the United Kingdom estimates that a 40-year-old woman wanting to retire on £15,000 a year would need to pay £640 a month into a private pension, or £499 a month after basic rate tax relief.

1 Explore work opportunities before deciding where to live. The retirement location you are considering may not lend itself to a business of that kind and jobs in your field may not be available.

2 If you have a spouse or partner, make sure you discuss your plans and try to find common ground where each person's ideas can be accommodated.

CHARTING YOUR FINANCIAL FUTURE

*I*t is not too late to be financially secure or to improve your financial situation. No matter what your current situation, there are certain steps to consider taking if you have not already done so.

CHOOSING GOALS TO MATCH YOUR NEEDS

Even when you have retired, you have financial goals, but nearly every person's goals are different. Based on your vision of your future, consider the specific goals you want to set. For example, you may want to:

- Spend all of the money you have by the time you die.
- Live frugally and build an estate for your children, a friend, or a charity.
- Pay for a grandchild's education.
- Donate money annually.

Retired people also differ in one other important respect. Some have saved, invested, and planned well for retirement; others have not. Even people who earned similar amounts during their lifetime and had similar family obligations may have very different amounts of money to manage in retirement. Retired people do, however, have at least one thing in common. They all want to be financially secure.

SETTING YOUR PRIORITIES

Even though priorities differ among retired people, everyone must decide what is important to them. Some people rank gourmet dining as a priority, while others are content with takeaway fish and chips. Some retired people want to travel the world, while others are content with the comfort of their living room. Set your priorities and manage your money accordingly.

Make your priorities in retirement compatible with your money management strategy. If you like travelling extensively, for example, having a large, expensive home may not be as important, which means you can trade down. If being charitable is a priority, volunteer your time in lieu of money gifts.

UNDERSTANDING THE RISKS

Strategies for managing your money rely heavily on understanding and feeling comfortable with risks. Every investment carries some kind of risk. Even failing to invest is risky because you could well lose purchasing power every year to inflation. Most of all, no investment is worth having if you worry about it constantly. Make sure you are fully aware of your ability to deal with the fluctuations in value that come with higher-risk investments.

DIVERSIFYING YOUR ASSETS

There are no guarantees when it comes to investing. Not many of us can predict the next boom sector of the economy, or which shares will go through the roof. You can, however, hedge your bets by having a good mix of investments. Most retired people should consider a diversified portfolio made up of shares, bonds, property, and cash.

▼ GETTING YOUR FINANCES INTO LINE
You need to get all your finances organized in order to have a comfortable retirement. Now is the time to be making those arrangements.

3 Retirement gives you a lot of time to sit on your hands and do nothing if you choose. However, you still need to remain active when it comes to looking after your money.

MAKING A WILL AND TAX PREPARATIONS

Retired people can differ enormously in their approach to preparing for death. Some do not want to deal with death or even discuss it. Others sort out every detail from picking a burial plot to selecting a coffin. As a minimum, every adult needs to make a will. Even if you do not think you are wealthy, inheritance tax planning can be beneficial. It may also make sense to ask a solicitor to prepare other legal documents, such as powers of attorney or a trust.

MAKING PREPARATIONS

Protecting what you have is more than just an investment strategy. It also means taking the legal steps necessary to protect your assets in case you die or can no longer care for yourself. Check your existing arrangements to see if they need updating.

CONSIDERING MAKING A WILL

No matter where you live or how much you have, you should consider making a will to ensure that your possessions are distributed to the people you choose. If you die intestate (without a will), intestacy rules will govern how your possessions are distributed, but a will avoids this problem. A will can also determine who will care for your younger children, assuming the other parent is unavailable.

Living will. This legal document is an offshoot of the will most of us consider. It permits you to state your wishes regarding life-and-death healthcare decisions, such as withholding or withdrawing life-sustaining treatment in certain circumstances.

DRAWING UP A WILL

If you die without a will, there are strict rules on who gets what. These vary across the United Kingdom, so check with a solicitor if necessary. However, it means that making a will ought to be a priority. It does not have to be expensive and you do not have to use a solicitor to draft the will. Many stationery shops sell will-writing packs, but be careful about using the DIY route. Wills can be more complex than they appear, and one that has been drawn up incorrectly will cause heartache and problems for your loved ones after you die. A simple will drawn up by a solicitor should not be expensive: they usually start from around £60 upwards.

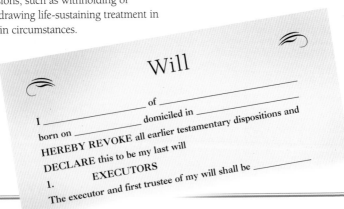

Will

I _____ of _____

born on _____ domiciled in _____

HEREBY REVOKE all earlier testamentary dispositions and

DECLARE this to be my last will

EXECUTORS

1.

The executor and first trustee of my will shall be _____

KEEPING RELATIVES INFORMED

Life will be easier for yourself and loved ones if you keep a list with at least these items on it:

- The names, addresses, and telephone numbers of all financial, legal, and other advisers.
- All account names, numbers, and locations of your investments.
- All of your creditors.
- The location of your will and the name(s) of your executor(s).
- Safe deposit boxes and where they are located.

UNDERSTANDING POWERS OF ATTORNEY

There are two basic kinds of legal documents called powers of attorney.

Power of attorney. With this, you authorize another person or organization to act on your behalf in a variety of legal and financial situations. It is no longer valid if you die or become incapacitated.

You can limit the time to a week or even a day and also limit its powers to a particular purpose, such as the power to sign a specific contract.

Enduring power of attorney (EPA). This gives the person you designate the authority to manage your financial affairs if you become incapacitated. If you have not set up an enduring power of attorney in advance, your financial affairs will have to be overseen by a receiver appointed by the court of protection. It is much more costly and unwieldy than setting up an enduring power of attorney beforehand.

THINGS TO KNOW

- If your estate is small, talk with an independent financial adviser about possible tax implications for your spouse in relation to your personal, stakeholder, or company pensions. Even though there may be no inheritance tax implications, there may be income tax to pay on the proceeds of these and other investment accounts.

- No matter how healthy you are, it is important to discuss your estate with an experienced solicitor who specializes in this area. You should also get your provision for healthcare reviewed by an independent financial adviser specializing in long-term care insurance. Private medical insurance costs often increase sharply at around age 65, and you may have to readjust your requirements.

- If you have an employer's pension scheme, make sure you have a copy of your letter of wishes. This tells the trustees of the pension scheme who you would like to receive your pension when you die. The employer is under no obligation to abide by it, but they invariably do. Keep your letter of wishes with other legal and financial documents.

- Find out who your beneficiary is on every account. Review those designations in conjunction with your will and your overall plan for distributing your property.

- Name a contingent beneficiary or beneficiaries in case the primary beneficiary dies.

- Keep a record of these designations stored with your other important papers, not stuffed in a drawer.

UNDERSTANDING RISK

As you attempt to protect what you have, generate income, and increase your assets, you will be faced with investment risks. Learning how to cope with them will improve your chances of successfully managing your money in retirement. Here are the major risks you face.

LOSING MONEY DUE TO INFLATION

You can have a lot of money, but it is not going to mean much if the necessities of life cost more each day. Whether these are groceries or heating bills, it is difficult to cope with rising prices. You could spend 15, 20, or 30 years in retirement, so you should not underestimate the effects of inflation, however modest. If your savings fall behind, you will have less to live on.

CONSIDERING LIQUIDITY RISK

Any investment that fluctuates in value can pose a threat to the investor who needs cash at a particular time. There is a distinct risk that you may need to liquidate the investment at the worst possible time.

GAMBLING ON INTEREST RATES

Whenever you put money into a savings or investment account that pays a fixed rate of interest, you are taking a risk that interest rates in general may rise and you will be stuck on a lower rate, watching the value of your return effectively fall. It is not just savings accounts that can be affected, but Government bonds, such as gilt-edged bonds (gilts), as well. Gilts are often sold as a much lower-risk investment, because you get your capital back at redemption. However, if you sell the bond before then, you will be subject to the effects of interest rates. When interest rates rise, typically, many bonds will fall in value, because newly issued bonds with the same qualities will carry a higher rate of interest, and therefore will be more attractive to investors.

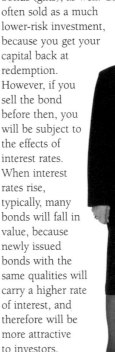

TAKING INDUSTRY RISK INTO ACCOUNT

You do not have to look back far to see how the fortunes of an entire industry can change. The TMT (technology, media, and telecoms) bubble, which burst in spectacular style in the early months of 2000, left many investors stung. When Railtrack was put into administration, many thousands of investors faced substantial losses. However, the ups and downs can be more subtle, and still have an impact on your savings. If you have invested heavily in one particular sector, you could see a large portion of your money affected.

RUNNING OUT OF MONEY

There are several reasons why you may not have enough money for your later years, when expenses can rise:

- Your investments do not keep up with inflation.
- You withdraw too much.
- You do not invest wisely.
- You underestimate how much you need in the first place.

HELEN'S
MONEY
1930–
2000

4 Every investment may have one, some, or all of the risks mentioned here.

RECOGNIZING CREDIT RISK

When you buy fixed income securities, such as gilts and corporate bonds, you are lending money to a borrower, either to the Government or a company. Credit risk is based on the likelihood that you will be paid back money you have lent in a timely fashion. The creditworthiness of that borrower (the credit *quality* of that borrower) determines the level of risk you are taking.

Generally, *issuers* (the ones who borrow your money) with the highest credit risk pay the highest interest rates to attract investors. UK Government bonds have almost no credit risk, but some corporate bonds may have a high risk that the borrower will default on its obligation.

ASSESSING MARKET RISK

Almost every investment has market risk and may lose value when faced with adverse economic conditions. The economic climate can affect even the bluest of blue chip shares, let alone a high-tech company or a start-up firm. Retired people must be aware of the market risk as they structure a portfolio for their retirement years.

DESIGNING A STRATEGY

*I*n order to achieve your financial goals, you have to make the most of the assets you have. Here are some ways to manage your assets effectively.

USING THREE MAIN STRATEGIES

Retired people are not a homogeneous group. Just as your aims may be different to the goals of others, your strategies for achieving those goals can also be different. There are, however, three general strategies to consider. Your own may involve one strategy or a combination of strategies:

- Live on your income without using your capital.
- Maximize your income, even if it uses all your capital.
- Grow your capital as much as you possibly can.

IT'S A FACT

The average personal pension plan is worth a total of £23,000 at retirement.

PROTECTING WHAT YOU HAVE

As a retired person, protecting your assets is extremely important. You are no longer at a job where you make more money each year. Instead of a salary, you depend upon the assets you have built up over the years. It is your job to make sure they are still working for you years from now.

When you are focused on protecting your money, the safety of an investment should be your most important consideration. Many retired people sacrifice their rate of return in order to have a very safe investment. What many overlook, however, is that their "safe" investments do not earn enough to keep up with inflation. In effect, they end up losing money anyway.

5 There are investment funds that are designed specifically to blend more than one strategy for people who do not have cut-and-dried goals.

6 Do not wait until it is too late to do your tax planning. Consider your tax situation before the end of the tax year for the best results.

OVERLAPPING STRATEGIES

Although your focus may be on safety, income, or growth, a particular investment may have objectives that overlap. Sometimes, retired people may need to settle for something less than absolute safety to increase income, but there are investments that can strike a balance between safety and income. Furthermore, there are strategies you can implement to reduce your investment risks. Talk to a financial adviser, if you have questions you cannot answer.

EARNING INCOME FROM YOUR ASSETS

The assets you have can be used to generate income. You are in charge of earning as much income as you can without putting them in jeopardy.

Retired people usually focus on income more than growth. They gravitate to income investments such as bonds, gilts, corporate bonds, and with-profit funds. Bonds are loans or debts issued by corporations or Government entities to raise money. The issuer of a bond agrees to pay bondholders a specified amount of interest and to repay the capital (amount borrowed) at maturity (the end of the loan).

GROWING MORE MONEY

Since retirement may last 20 years or longer, you probably still need to invest for growth. Otherwise, the income that seems sufficient today may no longer be adequate to carry you through an unpredictable number of years living your lifestyle. Younger retired people in particular should seriously consider investing for growth. Consequently, a retired person's portfolio may include individual shares and collective investments. Investing for growth is less risky when you have a long-term horizon, meaning you will not need the money for at least ten years.

PROTECTING WHAT YOU HAVE

There is one sure way to protect your assets in retirement: spend less than you are earning. Also make sure your investments do not give you a false sense of security.

INVESTING FOR PROTECTION

No strategy will guard against all risks, but buying a mix of investments (diversifying) can help protect against many downturns in the economy.

BUYING PROPERTY

Property has historically performed well against inflation. When inflation has risen, property has typically increased in value, outpacing the inflation rate.

You can invest in property and still reduce the risks by repaying your mortgage more quickly. This will increase the equity in your home, which has two positive effects:

- You will increase the cash you keep if you eventually sell the home and pay off your loan.
- You will increase the amount you could borrow at a later date. Perhaps you might want to buy more properties, in which case you may be able to increase your mortgage in order to release some capital to fund your new purchases.

OPTING FOR GILTS AND NATIONAL SAVINGS

For many older people, the security of their investments is crucial. If you want to hold on to the capital you have, bonds and products from National Savings and Investments (the new name for National Savings) may be worth considering. These investments are backed by the Government, and are easy to buy over the telephone or at your Post Office. The rates they offer are not always the most competitive, but some of the products are tax-efficient. Index-linked certificates, for example, offer growth at a certain rate plus inflation. They are tax-free and better investments for higher-rate taxpayers. Other investments to consider are:

Pensioner's Bonds. These are aimed at people aged 60 and over.

Gilts. These are not a National Savings product, they are UK Government bonds, which can be bought individually or within a fund.

---

7 You do not have to declare any index-linked certificates you own on your self-assessment form.

USING CASH-BASED DEPOSITS

The investment industry provides a range of accounts that are designed to protect your money as their top priority.

Bank and building society accounts. Putting your money into a bank or building society does not just have to mean opening an easy access account – there are many different ones to choose from, some of which pay a much higher rate of interest than others, so shop around. Fixed rate accounts are another alternative, but if the Bank of England raises base interest rates during the term, your rate may look less competitive.

Notice accounts. If you do not mind giving between one and three months' notice of any withdrawals, you can normally get a higher rate of interest with these accounts.

Money market term deposits. If you have a substantial amount of money (£50,000 or more) and you want to find a short-term home for your money (a minimum of one month), you could consider investing in a money market term deposit. It is a fixed-rate, fixed-term deposit account. Interest rates fluctuate, but yours is fixed at the time and date you invest. Rates are higher than on high street savings accounts, but lower than you could get on a longer-term deposit.

Understanding Trusts

A trust is a legal arrangement in which you hold property for the benefit of others (called beneficiaries). By setting up a trust, you can ensure your wishes are carried out after you die.

Using Trusts to Protect Assets

You can set up trusts to protect particular assets.

Fixed Interest Trust. With a fixed interest trust, you can pass a life interest in an asset on to a beneficiary. A fixed interest trust may be set up so that if one spouse dies, his or her life interest in the family property can be passed to the other spouse. The home itself would then pass on to the children when they reach a predetermined age (often when the children reach 21 years of age). It means that, even if the surviving spouse dies when the children are still young, the children cannot access the value of the property until they reach the age laid down in the trust.

Protected Fixed Interest Trust. This is a variation of the fixed interest trust and is designed for passing on assets to people who may find it difficult to make responsible decisions about money, or who may be reckless. If, for example, the beneficiary tried to sell property held in a trust, or remortgage it, the trustees could stop that person from doing it.

Building in More Protection

You can protect your assets further by setting up a discretionary trust. There are two types: full trust and A&M trust.

Full trust. With this type of trust, the trustees decide which of a number of named beneficiaries (or possibly a class of unnamed beneficiaries, such as grandchildren) can have income, capital, both, or neither. If the beneficiary does not receive income or capital, the money is accumulated. There can be quite severe tax consequences with a full trust.

8 You can put a wide variety of assets into a trust, so check with a solicitor or accountant.

9 Full trusts are quite expensive to run, so tend to be used only by wealthier families.

CREATING A SIDE LETTER OF WISHES

Trustees have a lot of power with discretionary trusts. They can make investment decisions about the money and run the trust as if it were effectively their own money. Solicitors would normally recommend that the person setting up the trust creates a side letter of wishes as well. It gives the trustees guidance as to how you would like the trust to be run, something they normally appreciate. Although a side letter is not binding, trustees will generally take notice of it.

WRITING A PENSION IN TRUST

If you have a pension, you can write the policy in a flexible trust so it goes to the person specified, and does not form part of your estate. You can set up a trust for occupational pensions, instead of relying on the letter of wishes, which may be better for some families.

PUTTING LIFE INSURANCE IN TRUST

You can take out a life insurance policy, written in trust, that is specifically designed to pay a potential inheritance tax (IHT) bill on your death. This is something a financial adviser will be able to arrange for you, but it must be done properly. An incorrectly written trust could actually increase the inheritance tax bill, so take professional advice.

A&M trust. The advantage of an A&M (accumulation and maintenance) trust is its flexibility. It allows you to leave different proportions of your money to different children. It also has fewer tax disadvantages than full discretionary trusts. An A&M trust is often used to leave money to grandchildren. While they are young, money will either be accumulated or partly used to pay for school fees and other expenses. They would then receive an income at 18, and capital or a life interest in the trust at 25 years of age. In order to set up an A&M trust, three conditions have to be fulfilled:

- The beneficiaries must obtain an interest in possession at age 25 or earlier.
- All beneficiaries have to be the grandchildren of the same grandparent.
- The trust must be irrevocable.

GETTING DISCOUNTS

L*ife has changed a great deal since you went to the cinema as a youngster and got a discount for being under a certain age. (Films have changed a great deal as well.) Today, discounts range from purchases on the internet to a free meal on your birthday.*

SENIOR CITIZENS' DISCOUNTS

The good news about getting older is that your age entitles you to discounts on food, shopping, and services. Do not be embarrassed to admit your age and ask for your discount. Here are a few:

- The Association of Retired and Persons Over 50 (ARP/050 – log on to www.arp050.org.uk) offers inexpensive membership to people who are 50 or older. You can then get discounts on computers, electrical goods, wines, and entertainment.
- Some employers offer discounts to retired ex-employees.
- Some restaurant chains give free drinks to senior citizens or a discount on the food purchased.
- Travel discount arrangements may vary between England, Scotland, Wales,

and Northern Ireland. For example, in England, men and women aged 60 and over are currently offered a minimum of 50% off bus travel, via a free bus pass. To get a third off rail fares, retired people must buy a special railcard. Also check with coach companies for discounts.

- You can get discounts at cinemas and museums, and on other forms of entertainment. You can also get reduced prices on haircuts and other services by showing proof of age.
  - Many holiday resorts and hotels will give older people a discount, particularly during the low season.

◀BEING RESOURCEFUL
You can find all kinds of discounts at all sorts of different places. Do not be afraid to ask if there is a senior citizens' discount. You may be pleasantly surprised.

LOOKING FOR DISCOUNTS

There are many organizations that offer discounts to their members. These are a few of them:

● Car rescue services have more benefits than just jump-starting your car on a cold day. Simply telephone them and check whether they have discounts on car insurance and car-buying reports, servicing, car hire, and attractions.

● Entertainment discount books are sold in some cities by different companies. They may offer two-for-one dining at selected restaurants, as well as at fast food outlets. You may be able to get discounts in shops and on hotel reservations, car rentals, golf courses, dry cleaning, and an assortment of other services.

● Many credit cards offer discounts on purchases and other incentives. Some offer air miles, and others even offer cashbacks. As long as you pay your balance in full each month and do not incur an annual fee, these credit card perks are attractive.

● You can buy a membership to a discount warehouse. You will then be able to purchase many items at a discount just by belonging to one.

 II To cut the costs of foreign travel, consider low-cost airlines or last-minute getaways. You can access them over the internet or by telephone.

 10 Always compare the prices and discounts before paying the membership fee at price clubs.

HELPING YOUNGER RETIRED PEOPLE

Younger retired people do not have to feel bad because they are not old enough to qualify for some discounts. There are other discounts available that are not related to age:

● Many restaurants offer early-bird dinners to people who eat before a certain time. You will sometimes find special prices if you eat out on a weekday. These deals will not be available on weekends, when the restaurant is typically more crowded.

● Get out those scissors and start cutting. You can find coupons in the newspaper and in direct mailings from retailers in your area. You can also print them off from the internet.

● Many businesses offer a discount for paying cash.

CUTTING BACK ON EXPENSES

Some of you may be able to look back fondly on the days when you had an expense account. Now all of those lunches and trips come out of your own pocket, but you can still enjoy a good lifestyle on a modest budget.

12 Miscellaneous expenses are often the problem. Take a week and write down every penny you spend. You will be surprised by how much you are spending.

EXAMINING LIVING EXPENSES

Initially, you need to determine how much your lifestyle is costing. Take a look at these expenses and how much you are spending on a monthly basis:

- Mortgage or rent.
- Council tax.
- Home maintenance and upkeep.
- Food.
- Clothing.
- Utilities.
- Car-related expenses (petrol, tax disc, repairs, and so on).
- Insurance (car, home, contents, and life).
- Healthcare expenditure.
- Entertainment.
- Travel.
- Loans and credit card debt.
- Miscellaneous expenses.

REVISING YOUR BUDGET

Retired people often find they are spending more in retirement than they projected. A miscalculation of 10% is to be expected. Here are some reasons why this happens. They have:

- More time to spend money and go shopping.
- More leisure time to become involved in activities that cost money.
- A greater tendency to splash out.
- More time to travel.

TAKING STEPS TO CURB OVERSPENDING

If you are over budget, you risk running out of money and may need to pull in the reins right away. Some people consider taking these steps:

Luxuries/necessities. Distinguish between items you must buy and things it would be nice to own.

Stop credit cards. Put away your credit cards to help curb impulse spending. Carry your credit cards for a planned purchase only.

Avoid ATM withdrawals. Decide how much cash you need and do not spend a penny more.

Buy right. With the right planning, you can buy most of the things you want at a more reasonable price. Thoroughly investigating each purchase can help you get the best value, or you may decide that a purchase is not worth the money.

Overspending. Do not overspend in one budget area without cutting costs in another. If you go on an expensive trip, you may want to cut costs by eating out less often or by renting a video instead of going out to the cinema.

Move or sell something. It may be time to move to a smaller house or sell that second car.

Coordinate. Make sure you and your spouse or partner (if you have one) have the same ideas when it comes to spending. Try to agree on a budget that both of you can follow without feeling deprived.

CHANGING EXPENSES

In retirement, some expenses are likely to go up, while others are likely to come down. Here are some expenses that may go away:

● Mortgage.
● Commuting costs, unless you get a part-time job.
● Work-related expenses such as lunches out or clothing.
● Financial responsibility for children.

However, there may also be expenses that go up, such as:

● Healthcare.
● Heating costs.
● Travel.
● Entertainment.

13 Leave room in your budget for unexpected expenses. You never know when the boiler will pack up or your car will need an expensive repair.

25

REVIEWING LONG-TERM CARE

W*hen you are managing money in retirement, a devastating illness can spoil all of your plans. If you need long-term care, in your own home or elsewhere, the costs can mount up.*

PROVIDING FOR YOUR FUTURE

Long-term care is ongoing care that assists you with the activities of daily living. There are three reasons why long-term care may become necessary:

● Ageing.
● Accident.
● Illness.

You should consider buying a long-term care policy for the following reasons:

● To preserve your financial independence.
● To protect your family from enormous long-term care costs.
● To avoid becoming a burden on your family and friends.
● To conserve your estate and preserve your spouse's income.
● To increase your chances of receiving your preferred choice of long-term care.

ADDING UP THE COSTS

Long-term care can be extremely expensive. Research consultancy Laing and Buisson found that the average residential care home now costs over £20,000 a year in London and over £14,000 for the rest of the UK. The average nursing home, which provides more nursing staff, costs over £27,000 a year in London and over £20,000 for the rest of the UK. The average stay in a long-term care home is 18 months, but stays can be much longer.

IT'S A FACT

According to the Association of British Insurers, only a very small percentage of older people in the United Kingdom have purchased long-term care insurance.

14 Long-term care insurance may be more important to women because they are more likely to outlive men and need nursing home care.

QUALIFYING FOR ASSISTANCE

The activities of daily living (ADLs) are the typical standard in a long-term care policy to determine whether an insured person qualifies for benefits. There are six ADLs, and the failure to perform a number of them usually means you can claim for long-term care:

- Eating.
- Bathing.
- Toileting.
- Dressing.
- Continence (the ability to control bowel and bladder function).
- Transferring from bed to chair.

DECIDING WHO PAYS FOR CARE

The rules about who pays for long-term care are complicated and discussed in detail later, but many people will not qualify for state help. Relying on the state will not give you much control about where you live. One advantage of a long-term care insurance policy is that you can choose the home you prefer. Care homes are happy to accept policyholders, because their ability to pay fees is guaranteed. Alternatively, you can receive the level of help you need to enable you to remain in your own home for longer. Social services currently put a cap on help within your own home.

RISING COSTS

Up to 1999, the cost of care in a home rose roughly in line with inflation, although some years saw higher increases than others. However, by 2001, many homes in England and Wales had increased their prices by around 6%, and some by as much as 9%. It is estimated that by 2012, the average annual care home cost in the UK could rise from £20,800 to £27,352 a year if inflation remains at 2.5% and care home fees rise only in line with inflation. If the prices increase by 5% a year, the average cost will rise to £35,568 a year. Many experts believe that care costs could rise by far more than the rate of inflation in coming years.

COMPARING PAYMENTS FOR LONG-TERM CARE

*A*lthough many rules relating to retirement are the same around the United Kingdom, there are some differences in payments for long-term care that could affect your retirement plans.

> **15** In cases where the state pays a contribution towards nursing costs, the money will be paid directly to the nursing home.

PAYING FOR LONG-TERM CARE

In England, the cost of nursing care in a nursing home is paid for by the NHS. It is available at different amounts, depending on the level of nursing care that an individual needs. In Wales, there is a slightly different system, with a flat-rate weekly payment towards nursing costs. Scotland pays for both nursing and personal care, with a flat rate for each part. Northern Ireland is also adopting a flat-rate payment system, with another, different, allowance for nursing costs. In each case, there are strict definitions about what counts as nursing care, so you may not qualify for a payment, or it could be at a lower level than you expect.

> **16** People with dementia-related illnesses often do not need much nursing care, but they do need help with personal care. Only Scotland pays for this at present.

IGNORING THE VALUE OF YOUR HOME

If you have to sell your home to pay for long-term care, you will not have to do it immediately. It may be possible to borrow money from your local authority, which must be repaid once you sell. Also, your home's value is ignored for the first three months after you move into a residential or nursing home.

17 You should contact your local social services department if you need help in arranging local authority funded care.

REVIEWING SAVINGS LIMITS

You have to pay in full for long-term care costs if you have savings, which includes the value of your home, above a certain level. These levels are often reviewed and increased and may differ between England, Wales, Scotland, and Northern Ireland. There are two savings thresholds: a lower one, above which you have to make some contribution towards care costs, and an upper one, above which you have to pay for care in full. Although your home's value may be taken into account, it will be ignored while your spouse or partner lives there.

PLANNING FOR LONG-TERM CARE

The fact that England, Wales, Scotland, and Northern Ireland each have a slightly different system means it is harder to make plans for long-term care funding. Some independent financial advisers have been reducing the weekly amounts that they recommend people must provide by the cost of nursing care that is paid in each region. However, it varies and since, in some areas at least, care homes have been effectively clawing back increases in benefits by raising fees, there is no guarantee that the amount your long-term care policy will provide will be exactly what you need. Many insurers have also promised a refund for policyholders if they take out too much insurance, and legislative changes mean more is paid towards their care costs.

GENERATING INCOME

No matter what your situation, you can generate more income and improve your finances. Even if some luxuries are out of reach, you can still have more things you want.

GETTING STATE BENEFITS

State benefits encompass much more than just a retirement pension. There are a number of other benefits that you may be able to claim, depending on your age and personal situation.

CLAIMING HELP FOR DISABILITY

Disability Living Allowance (DLA) and Attendance Allowance (AA) are the principal benefits that older people who are disabled can claim. You do not need to have built up a national insurance record to be eligible, they are not means-tested, and payments are tax-free. Disability Living Allowance is available to people who are aged under 65 when they claim and Attendance Allowance is available to people aged 65 and over.

ASSISTING WITH HEALTHCARE

Men and women aged 60 plus are entitled to free NHS prescriptions and sight tests. Younger people may still be eligible for some help. You can find out more by asking for leaflet HC11 from your GP or NHS hospital. If you or your partner get the Minimum Income Guarantee, you are both entitled to free NHS dental treatment, and other benefits.

IT'S A FACT

Older people miss out on over £1 billion of unclaimed benefits each year.

UNDERSTANDING RETIREMENT BENEFITS

Nowadays retirement benefits are not as straightforward as they used to be. The age at which women can receive the state pension is being raised from 60 to 65 over a ten-year period from 2010. People who delay claiming the state pension until after their official retirement date receive a larger amount when they do claim. Divorced men and women can collect a state pension under their former spouse's national insurance record if that person has made more contributions. The amount they will get depends on how long the marriage lasted and when they divorced. As well as the state pension, they may also get other benefits.

Minimum Income Guarantee (MIG). If you or your partner are 60 years of age or over, and you have savings below the current threshold, you could top up your income with the Minimum Income Guarantee (effectively Income Support for older people).

REWARDING SAVERS

Another benefit – a tax credit administered by the Department of Work and Pensions – is being introduced by the Government. The benefit, called Pension Credit, rewards pensioners who have saved modest amounts for their retirement through pensions or investments. It is not paid automatically, but you can apply for it. As an example, a pensioner couple with a full basic pension, savings of £10,000, and a second pension of £2,080 a year would receive over £600 a year.

RISING BENEFITS

Social Security benefits increase yearly by the same amount as inflation (the Retail Price Index) during the previous September. If inflation has risen sharply since then, you could struggle if you are on a fixed income. Income-related benefits rise differently – by the so-called Rossi index – which is RPI minus some housing costs. This means they often increase by less than other benefits. Inflation may not accurately represent the actual increase in individual prices because some items, such as fuel, rise more than others.

31

CONTINUING TO WORK

If you want to work after retirement, you can do so without risking losing any of your state pension. However, the rules are different with occupational schemes and there are restrictions about working and claiming your company pension.

DEFERRING YOUR STATE PENSION

If you are a woman retiring before 2010, when the state retirement age is still 60, you can defer your state pension up to age 65. If you are a man, it can be deferred between ages 65 and 70. For every year that you choose not to take your pension, it will increase by 7.5%. You are not obliged to defer your pension by the full five years, but if you have not already retired by age 65 (for women) or age 70 (for men), it will be paid anyway. It has been suggested that, from 2010, the deferment percentage may rise to 10% a year.

CHANGING STATE RETIREMENT AGE

Changes to the state retirement age for women are being introduced over a 10-year period. Consult the table below to find out when you will be able to claim your state pension:

Birth Year	Retirement Age
Before 6.4.1950	60
6.4.1950–5.4.1951	Between 60 and 61
6.4.1951–5.4.1952	Between 61 and 62
6.4.1952–5.4.1953	Between 62 and 63
6.4.1953–5.4.1954	Between 63 and 64
6.4.1954–5.4.1955	Between 64 and 65
After 5.4.1955	65

LOOKING AT OCCUPATIONAL PENSIONS

Under current rules, you cannot work part-time for the same company that pays you a pension. This has created a retention problem for a number of industries, where people at retirement age either go and work for the nearest competitor, because their skills will be transferable, or they work on a consultancy basis, without having the same obligations to the firm.

18 Good reasons for working in retirement include extra money, keeping active, preventing boredom, staying sharp, and staying sociable.

TURNING A HOBBY INTO A BUSINESS

One reason why people retire is that they have dreams of devoting more time to hobbies and activities they love. Some hobbies have the potential to earn money if you turn them into a business. You need to ask yourself these questions before turning a hobby into a business:

- Will I enjoy the hobby as much if I am working at it full-time?
- Will the business prevent me from enjoying my other retirement activities?
- How much money will it take to start the business?
- Will I risk any of my retirement assets to finance the business?
- How easy is it to start a business of this kind?
- What insurance do I need for this business?

STARTING SMALL AND HOME BUSINESSES

If you are running a business from home, it could affect your home insurance or mortgage (if you still have one), and even create a capital gains tax liability if you use part of the home solely for business. However, there are a number of expenses you can offset against tax:

- You can write off a portion of your home-related expenses, such as utilities.
- Some of your car-related costs may be deductible.
- Certain expenses, such as buying a computer, may be deductible.
- There may be opportunities for business-related travel.
- Certain books you buy and subscriptions will be deductible.
- Part of the interest on loans and credit cards may be offset against tax.

DRAWING YOUR PENSION

N ow that it is time to consider tapping into your pension plans, make sure you understand the regulations relating to pensions and tax in order to get the best out of the money you have saved.

CONSIDERING TAXES

Many people do not realize that all the income they receive from private pensions, whether personal or occupational, is taxable. The only part of the fund that is not subject to tax is the lump sum (the amount of which is limited) you can take at retirement. Most people choose to take the cash, because it gives them more control over part of their money.

CLARIFYING SCHEMES

Deciding which type of pension you have is not as obvious as it sounds. Your employer's pension scheme could be treated like a personal pension at retirement. This means you will have to buy an annuity when you retire. If you are in any doubt, contact your employer.

UNDERSTANDING SERPS

SERPS (state earnings-related pension) is based on national insurance contributions, but only for employees. The Second State Pension replaced it in 2002. People who are entitled receive it with the basic state pension.

CLAIMING YOUR PENSION

Group personal pension plan or personal pension. The pension provider will contact you three months before your retirement date and give you a valuation of your fund. If you retire earlier, you may be penalized.

Stakeholder pension. The system for claiming is the same as with a personal pension, but there are no penalties for taking benefits early.

Section 226 plan. This precursor to personal pensions is less flexible as to when you can take benefits, and the tax-free lump sum is calculated differently (three times annual income).

Additional voluntary contributions (AVCs). Many people have paid into pension top-ups offered through company pension schemes. There are two types: in-house (offered by the pension scheme itself) and free-standing (from an insurance company). You do not have to take AVC income when you claim your main pension. Anyone considering retiring early with a large AVC fund may be able to live on that alone.

19 Your 25% tax-free cash can work even harder if it is invested in a tax-efficient way.

INVESTING TO TAKE BENEFITS

Many people think that saving in a pension is something you can do only years in advance. However, you can do some last-minute pension planning, through "immediate vesting", and it can be very efficient for tax purposes. If you use some of your tax-free lump sum, the tax benefits increase further. You simply invest a lump sum into a pension, on which you get tax relief at your highest rate. You are then able to take 25% of the money as a tax-free lump sum, to invest elsewhere or spend.

20 You can take benefits from your personal or stakeholder pension from age 50, but with a section 226 plan you have to be at least 60 years of age.

CONSIDERING YOUR ANNUITY OPTIONS

Under current rules, you have to use your pension fund to buy an annuity by your 75th birthday at the latest. There are two disadvantages to this. The first disadvantage is that if you die soon after retirement, the annuity provider gets to keep your pension fund (although it will also pay an income for life, no matter how long you live). The other disadvantage is that your retirement income will be tied to an annuity rate at the time you buy. Since annuity rates have fallen, many people have been disappointed at how little their pension fund will buy for them. If you have a large enough pension fund (many experts suggest £200,000 or more), you can delay annuity purchase.

Income drawdown. With income drawdown, your fund is invested to grow and provide you with an income every year. The idea is that it grows by enough to give you at least as large an annuity when you finally buy – when annuity rates may be higher. You should seek expert advice about this, because it can be higher risk and costly.

UNDERSTANDING EMPLOYER PLANS

*T*raditionally, occupational and company pension schemes have been based on the salary you earn at retirement. Some employers are now replacing those with schemes where they simply make a contribution into a pension fund on your behalf. Either way, you will still have choices to make at retirement.

21 If you have lost track of your occupational pensions, log on to www.opra.gov.uk and download a tracing form.

DECIDING TO WORK PART-TIME

Take advice before you go part-time. Some final salary schemes base your pension on your last year's pay, while others use an average of three out of your last ten years. Either way, your pension could be reduced. Money purchase schemes do not have the same problem.

TAKING A TAX-FREE LUMP SUM

You can take a tax-free lump sum at retirement with final salary schemes. The amount varies from scheme to scheme, but it is typically up to one-and-a-half times your pensionable salary. Your pensionable salary may be considerably lower than your annual pay, so check with the pension trustees.

INVESTING IN MONEY PURCHASE PENSION SCHEMES

Money purchase pension schemes are becoming more popular with employers. A money purchase pension is still classed as an occupational pension scheme, but your employer simply agrees to pay a percentage of your salary into a pension scheme. As an employee, you will also have to make a contribution and the amount you get at retirement depends on how the pension fund has performed, as well as how much was paid into it on your behalf throughout your career. Unlike with a final salary pension, there is no guarantee about how much you will receive at retirement and some employers, when introducing money purchase schemes, take the opportunity of cutting the amount they contribute.

TAKING A MAXIMUM MONTHLY INCOME

You do not have to take any money as a lump sum, you can have it all paid as monthly income. You will have less flexibility and you could get a higher return from investing your tax-free lump sum, but you will have certainty. Another option is to transfer your employer's pension scheme to a private plan. You will be giving up certainty, but you will have more flexibility and control over your money. However, it is definitely not suited to everyone. It is a complex area and you must exercise caution and get professional advice.

22 Money purchase pensions have to be used to buy an annuity, but your employer may impose certain conditions on what you buy.

CALCULATING YOUR PENSION

Final salary pensions pay a fraction of your wages – normally 1/60th or 1/80th for every year you have been a member of the scheme. The maximum pension you can earn is two-thirds of your final salary. However, for that you would have to have been a member of a 1/60th scheme for 40 years. Bear in mind that overtime, bonuses, shift allowances, and benefits in kind are not classed as pensionable salary.

TAKING EARLY RETIREMENT

Many schemes set a retirement date of 60, but it could be 65. Your employer may let you retire before then, without reducing your annual pension, but if not, bear in mind the impact that early retirement may have. If you retire five years early, you could lose 30% of your pension. If you know you are going to retire early, top up your pension to make up the difference.

EXPLORING TAX ISSUES

N*ow that you have retired, it is time to take an income from your investments, and boost the amount you are getting from your pensions.*

CONSIDERING TAXES ON INVESTMENTS

Your money could go further if you consider the impact of taxes. Different investments attract different taxes. Some will have tax deducted, while others are paid free of tax.

Pension plans. Income from state, occupational, and personal or stakeholder pensions is taxable and will be paid with tax already deducted.

Bank and building society accounts. Interest is paid net of basic rate tax. There will be further tax to pay if you are a higher rate taxpayer. Non-taxpayers can ask for interest to be paid gross, before tax has been deducted, by filling in form R85 (which is available in branches). You can reclaim tax already deducted by filling in form R40.

Gilts. Income is normally paid before tax has been deducted (although you can choose to have it paid after tax if you wish). Even if tax has been deducted, it will have been taken at the basic rate only, so high rate taxpayers will have more tax to pay.

Unit trusts or OEICs. Tax has already been deducted, but higher rate taxpayers will have additional tax to pay.

Individual savings accounts (ISAs). Income (and gains) are free of tax.

Share dividends. These are paid after basic rate tax. Higher rate taxpayers must pay the additional tax.

Investment bonds. Basic rate tax is paid within the fund. You can withdraw 5% a year. Higher rate taxpayers can defer the extra tax until maturity.

National savings. Products such as premium bonds, fixed interest and index-linked savings certificates, and children's bonus bonds are tax-free. Others have basic rate tax deducted.

Annuities (purchased life). Income is paid net of tax at your highest rate.

GETTING TAX BREAKS

Make sure that you are getting the correct personal allowances from the Inland Revenue. When you reach the age of 65, your personal allowance increases. If you do not receive notice of a higher personal allowance, contact your local tax office and check that they have the relevant details. Personal allowances are often increased annually in the Budget and you can find out the current rates from your accountant or tax office, or the Inland Revenue website (www.inlandrevenue.gov.uk).

UNDERSTANDING INVESTMENT BONDS

These bonds have basic rate tax paid at source, but allow you to take some income without further tax to pay. You can take up to 5% a year, and defer the tax until maturity, or when you cash in the bond. They are useful if you want to be able to take some money without paying additional tax, but perhaps have used up your tax-free ISA allowance. Since you can defer higher rate tax for up to 20 years, investment bonds are often recommended for people who are likely to become basic rate taxpayers in the future. Investment bonds allow you to put money into a wide variety of investments, from equity-based funds to more traditional life insurance funds. However, there are other products that offer a similar range of investments; the main selling point of investment bonds is their tax efficiency.

Top slicing. If you are a higher rate taxpayer, or think you are on the borderline between the basic and higher rates, calculate how much extra tax you owe by taking the gain and dividing it by the full number of years the investment has been held. Add this figure on to your annual income. If you are still below the higher rate threshold, there is no more tax to pay. If there is, you will have to pay additional tax on the proportion of the entire gain that falls within the higher rate tax bracket.

QUALIFYING POLICIES

Certain types of life assurance policies are referred to as "qualifying". What this means is that no income tax or capital gains tax are due on payment of the proceeds, either on maturity or on the death of the life insured. The rules about what makes a policy "qualifying" vary between different types of policy and how long they operate. For example, for policies that run for at least 10 years, the premiums must not rise sharply within the life of the policy, but must be level or rise within certain limits. They must also be paid annually or more frequently. In addition, the sum insured must add up to at least 75% of the total premiums payable. Also, many qualifying policies taken out before March 1984 enjoyed tax relief. However, altering the policies means the tax concession is lost.

GETTING A FIXED INCOME

*Y*ou may have heard fellow retired people complain, "I can't afford that. I'm *on a fixed income". One reason your income is fixed is because you may be depending upon fixed income investments to provide steady income.*

EXPLORING METHODS OF EARNING INCOME

There are several approaches to generating income from your investments. **Play it safe.** You can invest for safety even if it means earning a low rate of return, but you might not even keep up with inflation.
Earn income. You might focus on income investments and try to maximize the amounts you earn. Be aware that bonds differ in quality (credit risk). Generally, the lower the quality, the higher the interest, and the higher the quality, the lower the risk. You could lose capital, although only low-rated bonds generally present a considerable credit risk.
Income and growth. You might look for investments that offer income and some growth potential. Typically, these are shares that pay solid dividends and represent companies with a solid business outlook.
Income and security. Preference shares offer ownership in a company with dividends secured by that company's assets. If a company is liquidated, preference shareholders will be repaid before ordinary shareholders. In exchange for this security, you typically lose most of the growth potential of ordinary shares because preference share prices tend not to fluctuate much.

USING SAVINGS ACCOUNTS

Some savings accounts pay a fixed interest rate. Alternatively, you could invest in a money market fund via a bank or building society. These offer fixed interest, but the minimum investment can be very high.

OPTING FOR FIXED RATE BONDS

Most banks and building societies offer fixed rate bonds. Here you tie up your money for a set period of time, such as three or five years, in return for a higher rate of interest. They are not very flexible: you normally have to invest a lump sum up front and cannot top up your bond or take money out, without paying penalties. However, they can be useful for money you know you will not need for the term of the bond and non-taxpayers can ask for interest to be paid with no tax deducted, by filling in form R85. National Savings also offers various fixed rate products, such as the Pensioner's Bond, which offers monthly interest for two or five years to the over-60s, or fixed rate bonds that have terms of between one and three years, with interest paid monthly or annually.

UNDERSTANDING BONDS

A bond is actually a loan, which investors make to a company or the Government, that pays a stated return over a specified period of time. When thinking of a conservative way to generate income for retirement, most investors think of bonds.

Gilts. These bonds can last for a few months or many years. Short-term gilts last up to five years, medium term 5–15 years, and long-term 15 years or more. You can buy them by post (forms are available at post offices), and through banks, building societies, stockbrokers, and financial advisers. If interest rates go up after buying them and you want to sell, you will be selling them at a discount from face value. If interest rates go down, you would be able to sell them at more than face value.

Corporate bonds. With these, you are lending money to a company. Since they are not backed by the full faith and credit of the Government, they pay a higher interest rate than UK Government bonds. Corporate bonds differ greatly in quality. Lower-quality bonds, sometimes called junk bonds, pay a higher rate, but pose a greater risk of default.

Local authority bonds. Some local authorities issue bonds in the same way the Government issues gilts. However, you should be aware that they do not carry the same level of security (for which you will get a higher rate of interest). The amount of interest is fixed for the term, which is often up to five years. Basic rate taxpayers have no further tax to pay on income.

WEIGHING THE RISKS OF BONDS

Buying a bond sounds risk-free, but there are reasons why it is not. Suppose you buy a £50,000 bond that pays 5% interest until it matures in 25 years. Here are some of the dangers you could encounter:

- **You may want to sell the bond before it matures.** If investors can get more than 5% somewhere else, your bond is not worth as much. You will have to accept a lower price to make up for the fact that it pays less than the going rate of interest. However, if interest rates in general are lower than what your bond is paying, you will receive more than the face value of the bond.

- **There is a credit risk with certain bonds.** The entity responsible for paying you interest, as well as the capital at maturity, may run into financial problems.

- **You also risk losing ground to inflation.** In 25 years, that £50,000 will not have the same purchasing power as it does now. Time erodes the value of your capital. If the interest from bonds is your only income, your standard of living will suffer as consumer prices rise.

- **The bond may be callable.** This means the issuer can redeem it before maturity.

EXPLORING BOND FUNDS

*L*ike other kinds of collective funds, bond funds pool
money from many investors and create a diversified
portfolio. The fund manager decides which bonds to buy
and sell and when to buy and sell them. The parameters
for these buy and sell decisions must be in compliance
with the fund's investment objective, which can be found
in the information pack.

UNDERSTANDING BOND FUNDS

You can buy or sell units in a bond fund at any time. Bonds are normally held within a unit trust when they are part of a fund, and units in a unit trust are bought and sold at different prices (you buy at the offer price and sell at the bid price). This means that, when you sell, you may get back less than you expect. In addition, the value of your units (and the bond fund in general) fluctuates on a daily basis and trades are normally carried out by bond fund providers at certain times of the day. Although each bond within a fund (whether it is a gilt or a corporate bond) pays a fixed income, the overall income level of the fund can vary. On an ongoing basis, the fund manager will sell bonds at a gain or loss to create cash to reinvest in more attractive bonds. In addition, some bonds will mature (end). The cash returned to the fund by the bond issuer will be reinvested in other bonds at different interest rates and prices. These factors, plus others such as interest rates, cause fluctuations in the value of your units.

◀ **PUTTING FUNDS IN A POOL**
UK bond funds are not limited to accepting money from investors living here – overseas investors can also pay into one. However, there may be tax implications in the investor's country of residence, so it is worth checking these out first.

SELECTING THE RIGHT BOND FUND

There are numerous categories of bond funds. Some bond funds blend bonds of various types, such as corporate and Government bonds, either to lower the risk level or increase the return. Here are some of the major categories.

Corporate bond funds. These consist of bonds issued by companies. They can range from investment grade bonds, through to junk bonds. A higher headline interest rate is not the sign of a better performing fund – it is far more likely that it has invested in higher-risk bonds. There are many different corporate bond funds available, and it can be quite difficult to compare them. It is important to make sure that the investment objectives of the fund you have chosen match closely with your own aims.

High-yield bond funds. These invest in riskier companies: the higher the yield, the higher the risk to your capital. They also tend to react to changes such as interest rate fluctuations more like a share than a gilt. High-yield bonds can be useful for boosting income, but should not make up the majority of a bond portfolio.

Gilt funds. The fund will invest in a variety of gilts, with the aim of spreading risk and maximizing the income, but it is a more expensive way of investing than simply buying the gilts directly. The advantage is that you can buy into a diversified portfolio of gilts, rather than just a handful. Also, the fund may perform well enough to offset the effect of the management charges.

WEIGHING BENEFITS OF BOND FUNDS

Here are some advantages of owning a bond fund:
- You can buy units for a relatively small amount.
- You can arrange for the fund to pay you income twice a year, sometimes more.
- You can reduce your risk when purchasing high-yield junk bonds because of the diversification that comes with buying a pooled fund.

Here are some disadvantages of owning a bond fund:
- The annual expenses of the fund reduce your rate of return.
- With individual bonds, you can lock in an income stream. With a bond fund, the actual income may fluctuate because of different bonds held within the fund.

23 Corporate bond funds vary widely, both in terms of the types of bonds in which they invest and their overall income-producing aims.

BUYING AN ANNUITY

W*ith some types of pension, you have to buy an annuity to generate an income stream. They pay an income for life, so it is a way of ensuring that you do not outlive your pension.*

UNDERSTANDING ANNUITIES

When you buy an annuity it is, in effect, your pension income. If you have a money purchase pension from your employer, a personal pension (whether a group personal pension scheme, or an individual one), or a stakeholder pension, you have to use most of the fund to buy an annuity by your 75th birthday at the latest. You effectively buy a monthly income in return for all of your fund. Also, your estate does not get any of your pension fund back when you die – even if it is within months of the annuity starting – although you can also buy a spouse's pension. With most annuities, once you buy you cannot change your mind.

CHOOSING YOUR ANNUITY

The annuity that is most suitable for you will depend on your attitude to risk and your personal circumstances. There are several options:

Level annuity. With a level annuity, the amount you get throughout retirement remains the same.

Index-linked annuity. Here your income rises by a fixed amount, so that it keeps up with inflation. You will obviously get a lower pension at first, which puts many people off. However, you could be living off your annuity for 25 years or more, so it is worth taking the potential effects of inflation into account.

Spouse's pension. If you do not opt for a spouse's pension, there will be nothing for your husband or wife when you die. There is a lot of flexibility about the level you choose for the spouse's pension, and while a common figure is 50%, the percentage is entirely up to you.

24 Annuity rates between companies vary widely and you do not have to buy your annuity from your pension provider. The difference between the best and the worst can be up to 35%.

25 Income depends on the annuity rate you get.

Assessing Investment-Linked Annuities

One of the advantages of an annuity is that it is guaranteed. When you buy, you know exactly how much income you will get throughout your retirement. However, there are other options if you are willing to take a risk, and those are annuities that are linked to equities or other investments. They are becoming more popular because annuity rates in general are at a low level. The two main options are:

With-profits annuity. Here your fund is invested in shares, bonds, property, and cash – as with a normal with-profits fund. It is riskier than an ordinary annuity, but not as risky as having your investments in shares. The performance is not just linked to the underlying fund, but also the financial strength of the company behind it.

Unit-linked annuity. With this annuity, your money is invested in a pooled equity fund. There is no smoothing of the effects of the stock market (as with a with-profits annuity). You have to be comfortable with the risk level: there is a danger that, if your investment does not perform well, you will not have enough income. Your mortality risk is shared – that is, it does not matter how long you live as an individual – which means your annuity will not stop paying you. However, the investment company may decide to lower returns if longevity, as a whole, is increasing.

▲ **CREATING A STEADY SOURCE**
The biggest attraction of an annuity is that it offers you a guaranteed, steady source of income that you can arrange to suit your individual life needs.

Shopping Around

Despite the fact that people can buy their annuity from any company they like, many stick with their pension provider. However, it is well worth shopping around: some companies give better rates to men, others to women. In addition, you may be able to increase your annual income by buying an "impaired life annuity". Put crudely, you get a higher annuity rate because you have a shorter life expectancy. However, you do not have to have a serious illness, because over 1,000 medical conditions (including high cholesterol level and raised blood pressure) qualify.

USING HOME EQUITY

E *ven if you are emotionally attached to your home, you do not have to say goodbye to all of those memories just because you need cash. The equity in your home can, instead, be a source of ready cash in retirement.*

CONSIDERING HOME EQUITY LOANS

A home equity loan offers some advantages. You have the choice of:

- Taking a lump sum through a second mortgage or by refinancing your first mortgage and taking out cash.
- Taking a flexible mortgage, drawing down money when you need it, and then repaying it as soon as you can afford it.

Age limit. You can often only borrow up to the age of 65 or 70 and will have to provide proof of income.

Low rates. Since the loan is secured on your home, the rate is typically lower than other types of loans.

Buying time. You must be able to afford the interest payments and, while there are circumstances when raising a loan could be a useful option, it is probably appropriate only for certain people.

> **26** Do not forget that when you borrow money against your equity, you are agreeing to a charge against your home.

SELLING YOUR HOME

You can raise cash by selling your home especially if it no longer meets your needs and you can downsize comfortably For example, you may sell because you:

- Cannot afford the upkeep or simply do not want the hassles.
- No longer have children living at home.
- Have lower income and do not want so much capital tied up in property.
- Want to move elsewhere, either to be near your family or to live abroad.

UNDERSTANDING EQUITY RELEASE SCHEMES

Equity release schemes enable you to unlock some of the value of your property, while still having the right to live there until your death. Home income plans, a type of equity release scheme, got a bad name in the early nineties because the mortgages offered were variable rate and, when interest rates rocketed, some people ended up owing more than the value of their property. Safeguards have since been put in place, but these schemes are still very complicated and are effectively a lifetime commitment. That means you need to take expert advice if you are contemplating it. The three main schemes are:

Roll-up mortgage. With this scheme, you take a mortgage on a percentage of the property's value. You make no payments and interest is simply added to the loan throughout your life. The whole loan, with the accrued interest, must be repaid when you die or sell up. Unlike with the other two schemes, you continue to own your home in full.

Home income plan. Here you sell part or all of your home and the money is invested in an annuity to give you an income for life. These plans are less popular now that annuity rates are low.

Home reversion scheme. With this scheme you sell part or all of your home in exchange for a lump sum.

Eligibility. Requirements may vary from lender to lender and from scheme to scheme. As a guideline:
● You must normally be aged 60 or over (although one scheme accepts applicants aged 55).
● You must own your own home.
● The home must be your main residence. You must live there for more than half the year.
● All loans against the home must be paid off before getting an equity release loan, or settled on the completion date.

Amount. The amount you can borrow depends on a variety of factors, such as:
● **Age.** The older you are, the more money you may expect to receive since it is likely to be paid back more quickly.
● **Value.** The more your home is worth, the more you may be able to borrow.

GETTING HELP

Lenders that are members of Safe Home Income Plans make certain guarantees. Borrowers have the right to live in the property until they die and the loan size will never exceed the property's value. SHIP members will also insist that people take legal advice first. Call 0800 3288432 for information.

GROWING WHAT YOU HAVE

Most retired people shy away from investments that will grow their money. They believe they need to protect their money at this stage of life. Growing your money, however, may make a big difference to your retirement lifestyle.

INVESTING FOR GROWTH

In order to reach your goals, you may need to grow some of your assets, instead of putting them into conservative investments. Here is why.

ASSESSING THE RISKS OF CONSERVATIVE INVESTING

Even with safe investments, you take a risk by investing too conservatively. Here are some reasons:

Inflation. Your investment may not keep pace with the rate of inflation. Even when inflation is low, you might lose purchasing power, leaving your income insufficient to support your lifestyle.

Exhaustion. You may run out of money. According to one insurer's life expectancy table, 62% of men aged 65 today will still be alive at age 82, and 30% will be alive at age 90. With women aged 60 today, 76% will live to at least age 82, and 50% will be alive at 90. If you plan for a short retirement and do not grow your nest egg, you may run out of money prematurely. Thanks to advances in medicine, you may see the day when your children retire and ask to borrow this book.

CONSIDERING INVESTMENTS

When you invest for income, you are usually lending money in return for interest. Growth investments involve ownership of an asset that may increase in value over a period of time. Shares are the most popular form of growth investment. When you become a shareholder, you assume the benefits and the risks of ownership in a company.

COMPARATIVE INVESTMENT PERFORMANCE SINCE 1945
– ADJUSTED FOR INFLATION

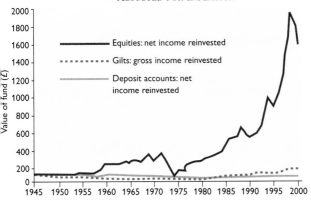

◀ COMPARING
PERFORMANCE
*Since 1945, in every
ten-year period except
1964 to 1974, shares
have outperformed
every other investment.
This graph compares the
growth of equities (an
equity fund up to 1962,
the FTSE All-Share
index from 1963
onwards), with net
income reinvested, to
long-dated gilts and a
savings account.*

CHOOSING TO INVEST FOR GROWTH

Many retired people are unwilling to invest to grow money. Here is why investing for growth is an effective strategy, even in retirement:

● You may still have a long time horizon. For example, some of your money may not be needed for five years or longer.

● Growth investments have historically provided the best long-term opportunity to maintain and improve financial wellbeing.

● You will have more money available for loved ones and charity. Even if you have more than enough money to support your lifestyle, growth investments probably got you where you are now and will give you a better opportunity to build your estate for the future.

LIVING WITHIN YOUR MEANS

Many experts say that to keep your assets for 25 years or more, you should withdraw no more than between 4% and 5% of your assets' value each year (plus an adjustment for inflation). However, you may find that this figure does not meet your needs, in which case you may have to consider other options:

● Cut your living expenses.

● Return to the workforce on a full-time or part-time basis.

● Increase your investment income. A different investment mix might permit you to withdraw a larger percentage.

27 Younger retired people, in particular, may need long-term growth investments.

REVIEWING GROWTH INVESTMENTS

When it comes to growth, shares (or equities as they are also called) and collective investments are the main vehicles investors use to achieve their goals. Be sure you understand what you are buying before you invest.

CHOOSING SHARES

Many companies are owned by people like you. To go public, a company divides its ownership into equal shares and sells them to the public. If you own its shares, you share in the success if it does well, and in the failure if it does not. In short, most people buy equities to let their fortunes ride with the fortunes of the company.

There are many types of shares. These types are not created to meet an investing need. Instead, they reflect the types of companies in the world and their various stages of development. Here are some of the different types of shares:

Speculative shares. These are start-up, or relatively new, companies who have not yet established themselves in

their product or service market. They may also be companies in high-risk businesses, such as the internet, biotechnology, and a number of other highly competitive and money-intensive industries.

Growth shares. These are companies that have moved beyond the phase of uncertainty and have proven growth patterns, but still have a lot of room to grow. The more and faster they grow, the more share price movement investors can expect to see.

Value shares. These are well-established companies with histories of consistent earnings and growth. Many value shares are also known as blue chip shares.

BUYING INTO POOLED FUNDS

Collective investments have a variety of investment objectives. Here are some of the possibilities if growth is your aim:

Aggressive growth funds. The fund manager does not hesitate to buy equities that are volatile or those with high P/E (price-earnings) ratios. This ratio compares the price of the share to the company's current earnings. The fund manager is looking for shares that have a chance to build a significant amount of earnings in the future. He or she is also looking for capital appreciation in a very short period of time.

Growth funds. These funds invest in shares with good prospects for future earnings growth. Although their futures look strong to the fund manager, the shares chosen usually have high price-earnings ratios and low dividend payouts. A growth fund manager may restrict investments to small, medium, or large companies.

Growth-and-income funds. With these funds, the fund manager focuses on two areas when selecting shares, the potential for price appreciation and current income. These funds typically try to create a balance between growth and income. They are often referred to as *balanced funds*.

Value funds. Here the fund manager invests in shares that are undervalued. The shares will have low price-earnings (P/E) ratios. Shares with lower P/E ratios are the most appealing to the fund

manager. A value fund manager may limit investments to small, medium, or large companies.

Index funds. Index funds attempt to mimic the performance of a market index, such as the FTSE All-Share or the FTSE 350. To achieve this, the fund holds all or a sample of the shares that comprise a particular index. Index funds are generally cheaper than managed funds because there is no fund manager.

Overseas market funds. These funds are for investors who do not want to rely completely on the health of the UK economy. The fund manager invests in overseas shares, for example in companies in Asia and America.

Emerging market funds. These may be even more volatile, because the companies they invest in are in countries that are less stable. These funds are generally considered riskier than overseas funds that invest in more developed countries.

28 Spread your money to reduce your risk. You should not put too much money into one type of fund or share.

MANAGING YOUR MONEY

You now have some idea of what types of investments are available to you. Next you need to select strategies that make you feel comfortable. This chapter will help you understand what is involved in selecting the right strategy for you.

WORKING WITH TIME

Just because you are retired does not mean you do not have time to invest for the future. With a little luck, you will have a long life ahead of you and your investments still have time to grow.

ASSESSING LIQUIDITY

When managing your money in retirement, you need to be liquid so you are not forced to sell off assets during a bear (falling) market. *Liquidity* refers to the ability to convert investments into cash without losing your capital.

How do you decide how much to allocate to cash income-producing investments that will sustain at least a portion of your needs for the remaining years? A good rule of thumb is to keep three to six months' worth of living expenses in ready cash, keeping an eye on interest rates. The remainder can be put in fixed term accounts, bonds, shares, and other investments that have the potential for appreciation.

CREATING A TIMETABLE FOR SHARE INVESTMENTS

The volatility of the stock market is most dangerous if you anticipate needing your money back soon. You risk cashing in at a bad time. Here is what many experts recommend:

- If you need the money within a year, consider "parking" the amount you anticipate needing in a savings account, not the stock market.
- If you have five years or more, consider putting some money in equities.
- If you have a ten-year window, consider increasing the percentage you have in equities.
- If you have over ten years, more of your money may be appropriate for investing in equities.

Everyone's attitude to risk is different, so take independent advice before you act.

COMPOUNDING

With time on your side, you can still take advantage of the power of compounding. Compounding enables you to earn money on your original investment and on the earnings from that investment. Time enhances the power of compounding. Your time horizon is the time between now and when you anticipate needing the money.

EXERCISING RESTRAINT ▶
The less you withdraw from your savings, the more you will have growing for you.

CONSIDERING VOLATILITY

Depending upon your perspective, volatility can be good or bad. The volatility of an investment is its potential for large gains or losses. Some shares go up significantly during boom years and down enormously during bad times. Some shares go down and never recover. You can never really predict what is going to happen. Those who lose the most are "forced sellers", who cannot wait for the share price to recover before they have to sell.

The more years you have until you will need the money, the less you need to be concerned with the ups and downs of share prices.

SHIFTING ASSETS

S ome people believe that the best way to protect money is by giving it away, but it can have long-term effects, so think carefully.

REVIEWING REASONS FOR ASSET SHIFTING

Shifting assets means moving them from one place to another. For example, you may choose to give some money to your spouse if he or she is on a lower tax bracket. There is also inheritance tax (IHT) to consider. Thanks to soaring property prices, many people now find that their estates are worth more than the inheritance tax threshold level, which could mean a large IHT bill. Asset shifting has been used for many purposes, both legal and illegal:

- Hiding assets from a spouse in a divorce action.
- Inheritance tax planning.
- Keeping assets from creditors and plaintiffs.
- Tax reduction.
- To qualify for benefits and aid from the Government and other sources.

SHIFTING ASSETS FOR TAX PLANNING

Asset shifting is an effective way to reduce the size of your estate and avoid taxes. Estates worth less than a certain amount are exempt from inheritance tax. Check with the Inland Revenue or your tax adviser for the current limit. The limit may seem a lot of money, but it is not if you bear in mind that the following assets are considered part of your taxable estate:

- Home.
- All personal property.
- Cars and other vehicles.
- Life insurance proceeds.
- Occupational schemes, personal pensions, and other retirement plans.
- Bank accounts, shares, and bonds.

▼ DECIDING WHERE TO STORE YOUR ASSETS

Most of your assets are probably in accounts of one kind or another. Think of those accounts as storage places for your items of value, each with a tag that identifies who has the rights to those particular assets. As your life changes with the seasons, you may decide there are advantages to changing your storage places.

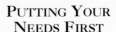

29 The rules on giving away money from your income can be complicated. Ask your independent financial adviser or accountant if you are in any doubt.

GIVING GIFTS

You can give away money to reduce your inheritance tax liability every year. The Inland Revenue sets an annual gifting limit, and you are also allowed to make a number of smaller gifts. In addition, you can give money away to your children and grandchildren when they get married. If you can prove you can afford it, you can also make larger donations, but they must be out of your normal expenditure. You can also give away other (larger) amounts through "potentially exempt transfers". However, for these to be free of IHT, you have to survive the gift by seven years. If you live for less than three years afterwards, your estate will have to pay the full level of IHT due, with the percentage reducing on a sliding scale the longer you live. Gifts to charity are always free of IHT whenever you make them.

PUTTING YOUR NEEDS FIRST

By giving away money, you can reduce your estate below the IHT threshold, but you may not have enough money for your own needs. This is especially true if you develop an incapacitating illness. Long-term care, either in your own home or elsewhere, can be very expensive, so make sure you have enough, should you need it.

LEAVING ASSETS TO YOUR SPOUSE

You can give assets to your spouse either when you are alive, or after your death. Both have tax implications. If your spouse is on a lower tax bracket than you, it can make sense to transfer income-producing investments from you to your spouse. If you are married, money and other assets left to your spouse are free of inheritance tax. What some people do is to leave the element that they have calculated will be free from IHT to their children and the rest to their spouse.

30 Some asset shifting is perfectly legal, while other manoeuvres are illegal and unethical. Make sure you understand the differences.

ALLOCATING ASSETS

F inancial experts recommend an investment strategy called asset allocation. To pursue this strategy, you divide your investments among different types of assets such as shares, bonds, and cash. There are several reasons why this strategy is recommended by so many.

MIXING INVESTMENTS

Your goal is to create a mix of investments that will be profitable over the long-term. By using asset allocation, investors can meet or exceed their investment goals with less risk.

Essentially, you are diversifying your investment portfolio, which is a way of reducing risk. However, it is not just a case of having a percentage of each different asset class. For example, the percentage of your portfolio in the stock market could be divided among different funds with different goals. There are several assets that belong in your portfolio:

● Shares and collective equity funds.
● Bonds and bond funds.
● Cash and money market funds.
● Property.

Reduced risks. Asset allocation reduces the risk that you have too much money tied up in one particular investment, such as shares. Since your portfolio is spread out among various asset classes, the odds are usually less that all of them will be performing badly.

DECIDING HOW MUCH TO INVEST IN SHARES

There used to be a rule of thumb that financial planners employed to determine the right mix of investments for a client. You subtract the individual's age from 100 to determine the percentage of assets that should be allocated in the stock market. With this rule of thumb, if you are 60 years old, 40% of your funds should be in shares, since 100 less 60 equals 40. A 40 year old should have 60% of his funds in shares, since 100 less 40 equals 60.

New ideas. That rule of thumb has lost favour, because individuals aged 60 or older cannot necessarily be too conservative in their investing. They may have 30 or more years ahead of them and need to invest to keep up with inflation. Nevertheless, older investors need to be liquid, so they do not have to liquidate their shares portfolio during a bear market. Another problem with rules of thumb such as these is that not all share investments are as risky. Investing in blue chip shares is usually considered a lot less risky than buying speculative shares.

CHOOSING PERCENTAGES

Supporters of the asset allocation strategy believe that investment success is not necessarily based on which investment you choose, but possibly more on what percentages you have allocated among the different asset classes – shares, bonds, and cash. Other types include property and hard assets such as gold.

The right mix of investments for you depends upon these factors:

● Your age.
● Your financial circumstances.
● Your risk tolerance.
● Your goals.

REBALANCING INVESTMENTS

Once you have the right mix of investments, you need to make sure they stay in balance. For instance, an equity fund may grow significantly and then represent too large a percentage of your portfolio. Rebalancing means selling some of the asset class that grows too large and buying more of the asset classes that are proportionately smaller.

UNDERSTANDING WHY REBALANCING HELPS

Here are two reasons for rebalancing:

● If your equity funds grow significantly, they may represent too large a percentage of your portfolio, increasing your risk because your portfolio is now less diversified.
● Your needs change. For example, the typical retired person needs a steady stream of income and may move some money to bonds and shares that pay dividends. As retirement age approaches, your investment horizon shrinks and it may be time to rebalance with an emphasis on liquidity.

USING A FUND OF FUNDS

A fund of funds can help solve your investment dilemma. Here, you get the benefit of a number of different fund managers, and do not just select the fund according to investment type. It means the investment can be more tailored to your own needs and goals. However, these funds can be expensive because you are paying two levels of management fee, so it is best to take professional advice first.

GETTING HELP

No matter how independent you are or care to be, do not be embarrassed to ask for help. Sometimes, this assistance will cost you money, but it is usually a good investment. Make sure, however, that the people helping you have your best interests at heart.

USING FINANCIAL ADVISERS

*M*any people can give advice *about financial products. Some have advanced qualifications, others do not. Retirement decisions are important and can be irreversible, so it is important to find someone who has the right level of expertise for your needs.*

31 Many advisers represent one company, so they will not be able to find the best product for you, from everything that is on offer.

FINDING THE RIGHT ADVISER

Here are a couple of suggestions to help you find a good financial adviser:
- Get referrals from family, friends, and business associates.
- Look at qualifications. All advisers have to take an FPC exam at levels 1, 2, and 3 before they are allowed to practise. However, some independent financial advisers (IFAs) have also taken a degree-level exam called AFPC. There are different elements, relating to specialisms such as pensions, tax planning, and investments. Certified financial planners are different to IFAs. They are also AFPC-qualified, but have taken additional exams, work on a fee-only basis, and are re-examined and licensed every year.

CHANGING THE RULES ON HOW ADVISERS WORK

Major changes to the way financial advisers operate and are paid are on their way. Under current rules, an adviser either has to be employed by one company (or work for it as an agent) or be independent. In the future, if proposed changes go ahead, advisers may be able to sell the products of a handful of companies as well. Independent financial advisers may be able to call themselves independent only if they are prepared to charge on a fee-only basis, should the client prefer that. It is likely that the biggest effect will be banks selling products from a range of companies.

32 Be wary of any financial adviser who seems to steer you towards one product, without taking account of your circumstances.

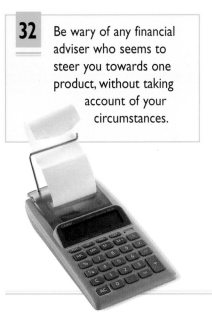

PAYING YOUR FINANCIAL ADVISER

Financial advisers make money in one of three ways or in a combination of the three:

Fee-only. Fee-only advisers earn no commission from the products they recommend and so may be less biased. Their fee is established in advance. You might pay by the hour or the session.

Percentage of your assets. Some financial advisers manage your portfolio and take a percentage of the assets they manage for you.

Commission. Some financial advisers earn commission on products they recommend. Although it may seem like you are getting free advice, you will not necessarily be getting objective advice. Your financial adviser may be inclined to recommend products that pay the best commission.

MAKING CONTACT

Here are some organizations to contact for financial advisers in your area:

● IFA Promotions: telephone 0800 085 3250 or log on to www.unbiased.co.uk.
● Society of Financial Advisers (SOFA): log on to www.sofa.org. This society lets you search for an adviser with advanced qualifications.
● Certified Financial Planners: telephone 0117 945 2470 or log on to www.financialplanning.org.uk.

WORKING WITH INSURANCE BROKERS

*I*n retirement, you still need to be absolutely sure you have the right cover
for your particular situation. You need to have an insurance broker who is
looking out for your needs, not his or her need to make a commission. Your
insurance portfolio can be every bit as important as your investment
portfolio. Take a look at your insurance cover in all of these key areas.

INSURING YOUR CAR

You are likely to be doing fewer miles in
retirement, particularly if you used to
drive to work. You may be able to qualify
for a low-mileage policy, which is usually
much cheaper. If you have an alarm or
immobilizer, you may get a reduction on
your premiums. In addition, many
insurers recognize that older people are
statistically less likely to have a motoring
accident. However, once you reach a
certain age (which can be 70 or 75), the
situation changes. Your premiums may
go up, or you could find it harder to get
car insurance at all. If you are driving an
old car that is not worth much, you
could switch from comprehensive to
third party, fire, and theft cover only.
Whatever you decide to do, make sure
your broker shops around because
premiums can vary widely.
It could be worth your
while approaching a
company that
specializes in
insuring older drivers.

EVALUATING YOUR INSURANCE BROKER

Good insurance brokers will have these
characteristics:

- They know it is in their long-term
  interest to find you the right insurance
  cover at the right price.
- They will not sell you any
  unnecessary insurance cover.
- They admit when you are better off
  using a policy from a different agent.
- They are every bit as helpful and
  responsive when you have a claim as
  they are when you are buying a policy.

G955 ERP

CHECKING YOUR BUILDINGS INSURANCE

Whether you live in a house or a flat, check that you have adequate buildings insurance. You should also make sure that you have enough insurance to cover rebuilding costs. Policies vary widely, so check the small print to make sure it is still suitable for your needs.

INSURING YOUR LIFE

Generally, your need for life insurance declines as you get older, since your children no longer depend upon you for support. It may be worth getting a professional review of your policies to make sure they are still suitable.

BUYING CONTENTS INSURANCE

Once you have retired, you may find the cost of insuring your home falls. That is because insurance companies count on you spending longer in the home each day and that cuts the risk. Some specialist companies that specifically target older customers may offer the best deals. If you think your policy is not competitive, ask your insurance broker to find a cheaper one. Some companies offer a no-claims bonus, which may even be transferable to a new insurer.

OPTING FOR LONG-TERM CARE INSURANCE

Long-term care is very expensive, and insurance policies that pay for it can be complicated. It is a specialized area, and not all independent financial advisers are aware of the issues surrounding it. Make sure you speak to an adviser who understands them.

CHURNING POLICIES

When an agent tries to convince you to turn in one perfectly good policy for another, the practice is called "churning". The agent gets a new commission when the policy is replaced and you may lose valuable benefits accrued under the existing policy. Replacement is good for the agent, but not necessarily good for you. In the past, some life insurance salesmen were criticized for churning endowment policies, but regulations have been tightened since then.

CHECKING PAPERWORK

Be careful when buying insurance over the telephone. Make sure you always check the paperwork carefully, including the small print.

CHOOSING TRAVEL INSURANCE

Some policies load the cost of travel insurance for the over-65s and most will not cover existing medical conditions. There may be exceptions if there has been no evidence of a problem for a period of time. Again, it is worth approaching specialist organizations whose services are aimed at older people, because they may not load premiums in the same way.

USING WILLS AND TAX PLANNING SOLICITORS

*I*t is important to make a will to ensure that your assets go to the people you choose and to avoid unnecessary tax liabilities. Office supply shops are filled with do-it-yourself wills and other legal documents. However, some matters should be left in the hands of the professionals.

FINDING THE RIGHT SOLICITOR

Whether you prefer to do it yourself or not, everyone needs a will. Unless you have the simplest of estates, you probably need the services of a legal professional as well. Furthermore, you might even need someone who specializes in estates and trusts, because some solicitors are not familiar with all of the nuances of inheritance tax planning. Here are some suggestions for finding the right person:

- Ask people you trust to recommend a solicitor.

- Look for someone who has extensive experience with inheritance tax planning issues and who specializes in them. The solicitor who handles your business affairs may not be the right person to help you with inheritance tax planning.

- All solicitors must have a practising certificate. Sometimes these have conditions attached that restrict their trading (such as not being able to handle clients' money). However, these need not indicate a previous complaint.

DELAYING IHT PLANNING

Generally, people postpone inheritance tax planning for several reasons:

- They think their assets are modest.
- They have never really added up how much their estate is worth.
- They assume they have plenty of time to begin the IHT planning process.
- They misunderstand how much of their estate may be liable for inheritance tax. Some people still believe that inheritance tax is due only on assets such as investments and savings accounts. They do not realize that the value of their property will be included. Alternatively, they may think that IHT is not due if assets are kept within the family when someone dies. In addition, they may believe the costs involved in IHT planning are too high to be worth it.
- They are afraid they will lose control of their money, and will be advised to give it all away.
- They do not think that much can be done to reduce their tax liability. Research has shown that those with very large estates often take expert advice to cut the potential IHT bill that their heirs would have to pay. However, people whose assets are relatively modest, but still above the inheritance tax threshold, are often the ones who incur the largest IHT bill.

33 Picking a number from a telephone directory is not the right way to choose a solicitor.

IT'S A FACT

According to the Law Society, only two-thirds of people over 60 have made a will.

ASKING THE RIGHT QUESTIONS

You would be wise to interview several inheritance tax planning solicitors before choosing one. Here are some important questions to ask in order to select the right person:

- Do you specialize in inheritance tax and wills?
- What percentage of your practice is devoted to IHT planning issues?
- What relevant qualifications do you hold?
- Will you work in conjunction with my financial adviser and accountant?
- Do you charge a flat fee or do you bill for your work hourly?
- How much do you estimate that my inheritance tax planning will cost?
- What information can I provide that will keep down the cost?

USING STOCKBROKERS

Thanks to the internet, many people are becoming extremely knowledgeable about companies and investments. Some are researching investment opportunities themselves and even trading shares on the internet. However, a lot of people still rely on others for help in making their investment decisions.

UNDERSTANDING STOCKBROKERS

The number of trades carried out over the internet has increased sharply. According to the share ownership organization Proshare, in March 1999 the number of internet trading accounts stood at 40,203. Less than two years later, by February 2001, the figure had increased to 399,155. However, in spite of the increasing popularity of internet trading, many people still turn to traditional stockbrokers for assistance. Stockbrokers earn most of their living from commissions, and there are three types:

● Discretionary brokers – these are authorized to do the deals on your behalf, but will often consider only portfolios of £50,000 or more.
● Advisory brokers – these brokers will advise you on which investments to buy and sell.
● Execution-only brokers carry out trades according to your instructions.

CARING FOR YOUR INVESTMENTS

Under regulations governing the industry, advisory brokers have a duty of care over your investments. That means they should never advise you to buy or sell shares if they do not believe it would be in your best interests to do so. An investment recommendation should:
● Be consistent with your risk objectives and timescale.
● Fit in with overall asset allocation.
You can insist on any investment you like, but a broker who gives advice must warn you when an investment is unsuitable for you.

IT'S A FACT

There are currently around 11.5 million shareholders in the UK.

SEARCHING THE INTERNET FOR INFORMATION

You can use the internet for information on money management. Here are some suggestions:

- Proshare, an organization that exists to promote share ownership: www.proshare.org.
- Financial Services Authority (FSA): www.fsa.gov.uk.
- London Stock Exchange (LSE): www.londonstockexchange.com.
- Association of Private Client Investment Managers and Stockbrokers (APCIMS): www.apcims.co.uk.
- Investment Managers Association (IMA): www.investmentuk.org.
- Department for Work and Pensions: www.dwp.gov.uk.
- National Association of Pension Funds: www.napf.co.uk.
- Association of British Insurers: www.abi.org.uk.

CHOOSING YOUR STOCKBROKER

It always pays to do some research before you make your choice of broker, whether you are using the broker to carry out transactions for you, or depending on him or her for advice. When it comes to choosing, you may:

- Find your own stockbroker, through recommendation or research.
- Contact APCIMS, the stockbroker's trade body, for a list of stockbrokers. It includes information on what level of service they are prepared to offer.
- Ring the Financial Services Authority. Stockbrokers have to be registered with the FSA. You can ring 020 7676 0088 to make sure your stockbroker is registered.

SELECTING AN INTERNET BROKER

Nowadays, internet-based brokers are becoming increasingly popular, mainly because it is so much quicker and cheaper to trade. Brokers either charge a commission or a flat fee and, with some, the more you trade or the larger the size of your deals, the cheaper the transaction fee will be. It is not just the fee that is worth considering, however. Most trades are done in real time; with others, you may have less control about when they are carried out and therefore at what price.

65

PROTECTING YOUR RIGHTS

There are public and private groups that offer advice to senior citizens, as well as assistance if a problem occurs.

CONSULTING CONSUMER PROTECTION AGENCIES

These agencies can be useful if you are having a problem and cannot get it put right. They may investigate it on your behalf, or simply give you some advice.

34 ARP/050 is a leading voice for senior citizens. Call 0500 050050, or visit www.arp050.org.uk.

Citizens' Advice Bureaux (CAB). Your local telephone directory should give you the number for your nearest CAB. Their telephone lines can be very busy, however, so it may be easier to call in for some face-to-face advice. Alternatively, you can log on to www.nacab.org.uk. CABs give advice on all kinds of problems, including financial issues, welfare rights, and legal problems. Many CABs also have a specialist Money Advice service operating from the same office, which can give you free advice.

◄USING YOUR POWER
Just because you are getting older, it does not mean you are becoming defenceless.

Trading standards. If you have a problem with goods or services that you have bought, you can take it up with your local trading standards office. You can find the nearest one by logging on to www.tradingstandards.gov.uk and typing in your postcode. The site also has a wide range of advice leaflets to download and print off. Your local office can also explain your rights and how to get redress. In serious cases, they may follow it up on your behalf.

TAKING CONTROL OF MATTERS

Sometimes you will have to take matters into your own hands. Here are some avenues to take if you have been wronged and the consumer protection agencies are unable to help. There are normally ways to redress your legal rights without using a solicitor.

Small claims court. These can deal only with cases where you are claiming money or property worth under a certain amount. If it is a personal injury case, the maximum figure is even less. You can check the limits and get a claim form from your local county court, where you can set out the details of the claim, how much you are claiming, and from whom.

Financial Ombudsman. If you get nowhere complaining to your bank, mortgage lender, or pension provider, you can contact the Financial Ombudsman Service on 0845 080 1800.

Newspaper and television consumer or financial coverage. Look at the coverage that consumer or financial issues get in the local or national media. Some programmes and papers have a "case study-driven" agenda. That means they may be happy to follow up your story and try to get redress for you. Exposure in the media can be a speedy way of getting redress, but you should expect to be photographed or interviewed.

CONTACTING OTHER ORGANIZATIONS

There are other organizations that may be able to help:

Consumer's Association. The CA has new powers and, while it does not usually handle individual complaints, it can take action if it believes there is a significant problem. You can log on to www.which.net, or if you are a member, call 0800 252100 for advice.

Help the Aged. This organization's website has a range of useful information, from campaign news to fact sheets that can be downloaded. Log on to www.helptheaged.org.uk. It also runs Seniorline, a telephone helpline that gives advice and information. Telephone 0808 800 6565.

Age Concern. Like Help the Aged, Age Concern also has a very useful website with fact sheets and an information line. Day centres also have information leaflets. Log on to www.ace.org.uk, or telephone 0800 009966.

USING GOVERNMENT AGENCIES

Financial Services Authority (FSA). This organization regulates almost all of the financial products that are sold (although currently there are exclusions, such as some insurance products and bank accounts). Its website has a consumer help section, where it gives advice on how to complain successfully. Log on to www.fsa.gov.uk.

FINDING OTHER HELP

There are state benefits designed to help you in particularly difficult circumstances, for example if you become widowed. However, there is other financial help or community support that many people may be able to get. In recent years, the Government has also increased the amount of money available to help pensioners with heating costs.

HELPING THE BEREAVED

Several benefits are available to people who become widowed. You will have to fill in a claim form to receive a payment.

Bereavement benefit. This benefit is paid in the form of a tax-free lump sum. It is paid to either spouse when his or her partner dies.

Bereavement allowance. This allowance used to be called the widow's pension and is payable for one year, at different rates according to the claimant's age. Anyone who is aged between 45 and state retirement age is eligible. The older you are when you claim, the more money you will receive. There is a substantial difference between the lowest and highest rates, however, so make sure you are getting the correct amount.

Widowed parent's allowance. In order to quality for this benefit, you have to have one child living with you and receive child benefit. Check for the current widowed parent's allowance and make a claim as soon as possible.

GETTING HELP ▼
If you have suffered a bereavement, you may be able to claim certain benefits. Check your entitlement, however, to ensure you are receiving the right amount.

IT'S A FACT

Cruse Bereavement Care (telephone 0870 167 1677) is an organization that offers help to people who have lost loved ones. It also has drop-in centres for support and advice.

CONTRIBUTING TO YOUR HEATING COSTS

Winter fuel allowance. This is a tax-free payment given to all households with at least one person aged 60 or over. Contact the Winter Fuel helpline on 08459 151515 for details.

Cold weather payment. During a particularly cold spell, older people who are claiming the minimum income guarantee may get extra help with fuel costs.

Warm front. People aged 60 and over can apply for help with basic insulation costs.

GETTING OTHER HELP

In almost every area, there are special programmes for retired people. Some require low income for eligibility, others do not. Many programmes have state funding; others are financed by religious and community groups.

If you are struggling financially, do not hesitate to see what assistance is available for someone in your situation. Check whether these services, or similar ones, are offered in your community:

- Meals-on-wheels.
- Adult day care.
- Free or low-cost transport to appointments with doctors or hospital.
- Assistance with tax returns (for people on self-assessment).

IT'S A FACT

According to Age Concern, around 70% of pensioner households currently depend on state benefits for at least half their gross income.

MAKING CONTACT

Here are the telephone numbers and websites of some helpful organizations:

- Elderly Accommodation Counsel (has a list of accommodation for elderly people): telephone 020 7820 1343 or log on to www.housingcare.org.
- Warm Front (Home Energy Efficiency): telephone 0800 952 0600 or log on to www.eaga.co.uk.
- National Pensioners Convention (a pressure group with local branches): telephone 020 7431 9820 or log on to www.natpencon.org.uk.

35 If you have not got access to a computer, internet cafés offer cheap internet access.

INDEX

ACKNOWLEDGMENTS

AUTHOR'S ACKNOWLEDGMENTS

Sarah Pennells is very grateful to many people who gave their time and expertise so willingly. In particular Anna Bowes of Chase de Vere. Thanks also to Andy Cowan of Aitchison and Colegrave, to David Long of solicitors Charles Russell, to Lyn Webb of Legal and General, and to Kirsty Edmonds and Chris Ellicott at Age Concern Financial Partnerships. As ever, Sarah is grateful to Lorraine Turner and Caroline Marklew of Portal Publishing for being so relentlessly positive, and to the team at Dorling Kindersley: Adèle Hayward, Richard Gilbert, Marianne Markham, and Sarah Cowley, for their continued help and guidance. Lastly, Sarah would like to thank her friends Sarah Tutt and Emma Daniel, for always being there when she needed them.

Marc Robinson would like to thank Dallas Salisbury, founder and president of the Employee Benefit Research Institute, as well as EBRI's sponsors and staff. He also wishes to dedicate this book to Zachary Robinson for his great patience and support.

PUBLISHER'S ACKNOWLEDGMENTS

Dorling Kindersley would like to thank everyone who worked on the Essential Finance series, and the following for their help and participation:

Editorial Stephanie Rubenstein; **Design and Layout** Jill Dupont; **Consultants** Nick Clemente; Skeeter; **Picture Researchers** Mark Dennis; Sam Ruston; **Indexer** Indexing Specialists; **Proofreader** Caroline Curtis; **Photography** Anthony Nex; **Photographers' Assistant** Damon Dulas; **Models** Harold Rose, Eleanor Rose, Liza Steixner, Mimi Lieberman.

AUTHORS' BIOGRAPHIES

Sarah Pennells is a personal finance journalist who writes for a variety of magazines and newspapers, and reports on BBC1's *Breakfast* programme and *It's Your Money* for BBC1 and News 24. Sarah regularly writes for the *Financial Mail on Sunday* and *Shares* magazine and is the personal finance editor for *The Lady*. She has also written for the London *Evening Standard* Homes and Property supplement and *Woman and Home* magazine.

Marc Robinson is a Founding Director of LEAP (Latino Education Achievement Project). He is also co-founder of Internet-based moneytours.com, a personal finance resource for corporations and other institutions. He wrote the original *The Wall Street Journal Guide to Understanding Money and Markets*, created *The Wall Street Journal Guide to Understanding Personal Finance*, and co-published a personal finance series with Time Life Books. He is also the author of the KISS guide on Personal Finance. In his two decades in the financial services industry, he has provided marketing consulting to many top Wall Street firms. He is admitted to practise law in New York State.

PICTURE CREDITS

Key: *a* above, *b* bottom, *c* centre, *l* left, *r* right, *t* top
British Coal: 68; **Credit Suisse First Boston:** 49; **The Image Bank/Getty Images:** Yellow Dog Productions 4c.